ASSISTANTS AND LEADERS

KAREN HAWKINS

ASSISTANTS
and
LEADERS

BUILDING EFFECTIVE MINISTRY PARTNERSHIPS

YWAM PUBLISHING
Seattle, Washington

YWAM Publishing is the publishing ministry of Youth With A Mission (YWAM), an international missionary organization of Christians from many denominations dedicated to presenting Jesus Christ to this generation. To this end, YWAM has focused its efforts in three main areas: (1) training and equipping believers for their part in fulfilling the Great Commission (Matthew 28:19), (2) personal evangelism, and (3) mercy ministry (medical and relief work).

For a free catalog of books and materials, call (425) 771-1153 or (800) 922-2143. Visit us online at www.ywampublishing.com.

To Peter Iliyn,
North American Leader of
Youth With A Mission

It has been my privilege and honor to be your
assistant in serving the mission for over sixteen
years. Thank you, Pete, for your patience as I have
grown and continue to grow in this role. I have
learned so much from watching you lead.
You are a great man of God
and a true friend.

partner: a person who takes part in
an undertaking with another or others
. . . with shared risks and profits.

New Oxford American Dictionary

CONTENTS

INTRODUCTION

I have often wondered if many elementary school students who, like me, were labeled "teacher's pets" were simply demonstrating the gift of assisting leaders. Looking back, I see a lifelong pattern of desiring to assist leaders. Even as a young adult, I was always looking for opportunities to help lighten the load of my leaders. In the local church I was drawn to serve the pastor and his wife, the leadership team and their wives, and the Sunday-school teachers. At a medical clinic, I supported the director. Then as I began training with Youth With A Mission (YWAM), my heart was drawn to assist the school leader. These last sixteen years, it has been my honor and privilege to assist the North American Leader of YWAM.

Being an assistant has become one of my passions in life, and I want to help others who have a similar life calling. I believe there are those to whom God gives special abilities to support leaders. As assistants, we have a distinct role: to help our leaders function well. We are not motivated by an attraction to a personality, nor is our work about gaining title or position.

Rather, assisting is helping make things possible, coming alongside, serving, being an "armor-bearer," partnering, and so much more.

Our work as assistants is powerful in the Lord's hands.

This booklet has blossomed from my experiences in assisting leaders and from my notes on a teaching by Dawn Gauslin, whom I greatly respect. Dawn has assisted YWAM's founders, Loren and Darlene Cunningham, for many years. I also received much help and insight from Kathy Griffith, assistant to the former CEO of Greater Europe Mission. We worked together on the first draft of this booklet. I interviewed many assistants from other mission organizations and ministries, and their insights are interwoven throughout this work. I gleaned other good content from books about assisting leaders and have referenced those works at the back of this booklet.

If you are an assistant, Part 1 is for you. Whether you think of yourself as a secretary, clerical assistant, executive assistant, or an armor-bearer, I pray that this short booklet will stir the gift that is in you. I also pray that you will be encouraged by how God has created you to advance his kingdom. My hope is that this booklet will encourage you to accept and function effectively in your God-given role of assisting leaders. Your role as an assistant will not look like anyone else's. Remember this, for it will keep you from taking on more than what God has assigned you or feeling that you need to be a superhero to fulfill your role. God qualifies you. He will teach you. He will guide you.

If you are a leader, Part 2 is for you. Whether you have an assistant or are looking for one, here are some aspects to consider. I pray that you will be encouraged as well, and that your partnership with your assistant or administrative team will be fruitful.

This booklet can be used for personal or group study. The points and questions throughout are starting places and are meant to be expounded on and discussed in greater depth.

God has a purpose for us, and he loves partnerships!

> *I cry out to God Most High,*
> *to God who fulfills his purpose for me.*
> —PSALM 57:2 ESV

PART 1

ASSISTANTS PARTNERING WITH LEADERS

QUESTIONS TO GET THINGS GOING

1. Think of assistants from movies or TV shows. List some stereotypes of what an assistant is. Give positive and negative examples.

2. What first comes to mind when you think of assisting a leader? Do you feel qualified?

3. In light of the definition of a partner being "a person who takes part in an undertaking with another or others with shared risks and profits," consider your role in assisting. What risks do you see? What benefits do you see?

4. Consider the image of a tandem bicycle. How does this shape your thinking about your relationship with your leader?

STARTING WITH THE INSIDE

*Being an assistant is like [being] a painter. I like to show
my painting but not my face.*
—ENKHSUREN ENKHTUR, ASSISTANT TO RON BOEHME,
YWAM PORT ORCHARD

*I am not fulfilled when I am leading. I only experience
fulfillment when I am in the background.*
—ANDY MILLER, ASSISTANT AT YWAM ORLANDO

My Journey

When I began assisting YWAM's North American
Leader Peter Iliyn, it was to be temporary. I was to
fill in for a few weeks while his former assistant returned
home to care for her terminally ill father. There was no
training manual and no time for instructions. My journey
had begun!

I cannot stress enough how inadequate I felt in this position. There were so many new things to take in all at once. I learned to lean into God for ideas, decisions, wisdom, and daily strength. It quickly became clear that to be an effective assistant I had to start with the inside—my own character and identity—and learn to care for myself.

Qualities of an Assistant

Character is our beginning point and our ongoing pursuit as we follow Christ. The character qualifications for assistants must match those required of godly leaders.

Why? Because we will be representing Christ, the ministry, and our leader. We will be in a place of influence for both the leader we are assisting and those around us.

With this thought in mind, read 1 Timothy 3:1–13:

> Here is a trustworthy saying: Whoever aspires to be an overseer desires a noble task. Now the overseer is to be above reproach, faithful to his wife, temperate, self-controlled, respectable, hospitable, able to teach, not given to drunkenness, not violent but gentle, not quarrelsome, not a lover of money. He must manage his own family well and see that his children obey him, and he must do so in a manner worthy of full respect. (If anyone does not know how to manage his own family, how can he take care of God's church?) He must not be a recent convert, or he may become conceited and fall under the same judgment as the devil. He must also have a good reputation with outsiders, so that he will not fall into disgrace and into the devil's trap.

In the same way, deacons are to be worthy of respect, sincere, not indulging in much wine, and not pursuing dishonest gain. They must keep hold of the deep truths of the faith with a clear conscience. They must first be tested; and then if there is nothing against them, let them serve as deacons.

In the same way, the women are to be worthy of respect, not malicious talkers but temperate and trustworthy in everything.

A deacon must be faithful to his wife and must manage his children and his household well. Those who have served well gain an excellent standing and great assurance in their faith in Christ Jesus.

What are the qualities of a leader? How do those qualities apply to assisting?

From this passage in 1 Timothy, we can say that assistants, like leaders, must be above reproach, self-controlled, hospitable, not quarrelsome, and sincere. They must have a good reputation, manage family well, not be lovers of money, not be malicious talkers, keep hold of the deep truths of faith, and be trustworthy in everything.

To these qualifications we can add some general biblical principles. Assistants should be people of prayer, be spiritually mature with an obvious love for the Lord and his Word, and be aware of the incredible influence of their position and take that responsibility seriously. They must be committed, transparent, and accountable to a local body of believers where they are nurtured in the Bible and their spiritual walk. They should be people who encourage honesty and transparency from leaders and receive correction without taking offense.

Likewise, an assistant may be the person the Lord uses to mirror the truth to a leader.

> *As iron sharpens iron,*
> *so a friend sharpens a friend.*
> —PROVERBS 27:17 NLT

Developing Godly Character

How do you develop godly character in the day-to-day context of assisting? Consider the following.

Walk in humility. You will not do everything perfectly, even though you and others may expect perfection. We must be quick to admit inadequacies and apologize for mistakes. Make sure your leader hears about your mistakes from you rather than from others. At times others will judge you unfairly. Don't let insecurity creep in. Be confident in your role. You are accountable to the Lord and your leader.

Be a servant. Have a heart to serve the Lord by serving the leader. An assistant continually seeks to be a Mary in a Martha world—cultivating godly character while accomplishing tasks and serving others.

> *Whoever wants to become great among*
> *you must be your servant.*
> —MATTHEW 20:26

Remember that you are serving the Lord and he sees everything you do. Assisting is often a thankless job. We can sometimes feel that we do all the work and the leader gets all the credit. Guard your heart against jealousy or judgments. Rest in God's favor.

> *May the favor of the Lord our God rest on us;*
> *establish the work of our hands for us—*
> *yes, establish the work of our hands.*
> —PSALM 90:17

Demonstrate patience. The leader does not know everything. Nor do we. Pray for wisdom.

Walk in grace. Know when to speak up. Learn to wait on the Lord in the midst of your day and the moment.

Be careful not to gossip or have an unhealthy curiosity. We represent the Lord Jesus Christ as well as the leader. A relationship of confidentiality and trust is crucial. We are privy to sensitive information. Only seek information needed to serve the leader better. But remember, information does not give you control.

Have a good sense of humor. Be free to laugh at yourself and with others to lighten the mood in the office.

Questions for Reflection

1. What areas or disciplines do you desire to grow in?
2. What other scriptures would you bring into this conversation?

A Distinct Identity

Dawn Gauslin, longtime assistant to YWAM's founders, once said to me: "Walk *alongside* the leader so the light of

Jesus can illumine both of you. We are working *with* them, not *for* them." This is critical for any assistant to understand. You and your leader are a combination of ministry gifts, and you are a team!

Second Timothy 1:6–7 says, "For this reason I remind you to fan into flame the gift of God, which is in you. . . . For the Spirit God gave us does not make us timid, but gives us power." The Greek word for "gift" is *charisma*, which means "a gift of grace, an undeserved benefit from God" (*Strong's*). Even your talents were not earned but given by God.

God's desire is to interact with his children. The power is up to God. Participation is up to us. It is our responsibility to participate and interact with God. When we accepted Christ as Savior, in that moment he lit a flame in us. We are to fan into flame the gift God has given us.

Assistants have distinct gifts and callings. Therefore it is important not to live in the shadow of the leader. Although there are some things we are not anointed to carry, we are a major contributor to the work. We have a significant and distinctive role. What we do at our desk makes an impact far beyond our office walls.

Questions for Reflection

1. What does it mean to "fan the flame"?
2. Why is this important in connection with being an assistant?
3. How will you do it?

Types of Assistants

The Bible mentions many titles and roles: king, servant, elder, deacon, and so on. Titles and roles carry with them different responsibilities and kinds of honor, authority, and anointing. They can be the basis of shared expectations.

Perhaps your ministry is more casual and so titles and job descriptions are seen as too formal or confining. We all want to preserve the value of relationship in ministry. However, the use of titles and roles is helpful in defining what is needed and who is responsible for meeting that need.

Consider the following titles in light of distinct gifts and callings. Which one best fits your desire to serve? (These definitions will differ in various situations and cultures.)

- *Personal assistant.* Provides support for the leader (usually of the same gender); travels with the leader; runs errands, including non-office-related tasks.
- *Clerical assistant (secretary).* Handles filing, data entry, general phone calls, and basic correspondence; this position is more mechanical and task oriented.
- *Administrative assistant.* Oversees and organizes the office, the schedule, and travel.
- *Executive assistant.* Anticipates the leader's needs, does follow-up regarding tasks and communication, prioritizes demands, keeps leader on task, and handles more private or sensitive information.
- *Project assistant.* Supports specific projects that have a defined goal and end point.

- *Accounting assistant.* Specializes in accounting and finance.

To this list we can add assistance by way of prayer and intercession. This is a more fluid role. It is essentially standing in a more concentrated role of prayer for a leader and the ministry. Sometimes those who are drawn to this way of assisting might not have strong administrative skills.

Beyond titles and job descriptions, it is good to know what strengths you bring to your assistant position. There are many tests that can help in identifying your natural talents and strengths as well as those of your leader (see Recommended Resources for suggestions).

Once you and your leader have taken these tests, sit down together and review each other's results. Discuss your differences and similarities. Use these insights to find new ways to help each other work more effectively.

Self-Care

Assistants soon discover that closure does not always come at the end of a usual workday. Visionary leaders often leave their assistants a myriad of tasks, some with seemingly impossible deadlines. If we take this all on ourselves, we'll be drowning in stress. Stress is a killer of joy and peace. It also causes physical and emotional trouble.

To assist our leader and the ministry well, we must make taking care of ourselves a priority. We cannot do our best if we are physically and emotionally tired. I have personally struggled with a tendency to overwork. I have had to draw appropriate boundaries after gauging what I can and cannot do. I also must remind myself often that my identity is not in my work.

The basic disciplines of going to bed at a decent time, eating well, and exercising on a regular basis are so important. Also consider the following strategies for self-care.

Know your job description. Do you know your responsibilities? From the start, ask for a clear job description and revisit it with your leader at least once a year. Consider carefully before you accept any new area of responsibility. We have the responsibility to bring new opportunities before God in prayer. Drs. Henry Cloud and John Townsend offer excellent biblical counsel in their book *Boundaries.*

Identify distractions. We need to be aware of distractions that can pull us away from the things we should be doing. Our heart as an assistant is to assist, and sometimes we can be taken advantage of. Others may ask us to do projects or tasks that pull us away from our own job responsibilities, causing us to work extra hours.

Be a learner. A leader needs the benefit of a skilled and experienced assistant. We want to exemplify both people skills and technical skills, remembering that as the leader's responsibilities grow, so do ours.

Be creative. Don't get stuck in the same old ways of doing things. Changing times and technologies require that we be open to new processes and procedures, especially if the old ways are no longer working. Be quick to ask, "Is there a better way?"

Seek personal growth. Being a disciple of the Lord is key for our self-care. Learning more of his ways and character and applying them in our daily lives will give us wisdom and strength to do our job.

Take breaks. Get away from your desk at lunch and take

quick breaks in other moments throughout your day. As much as possible do not work while eating. Consider going for a walk during your lunch break.

Take bigger breaks. Take two- or three-day retreats for spiritual renewal. Also, don't miss taking a yearly vacation. On your days off, use the other side of your brain. Pick up hobbies. Join others for bike riding, mountain climbing, running, swimming, discussion groups, Bible study, and so on. Learn what renews you and refuels you, and make the time to do it.

Look after your appearance. While this is an important part of being a good representative, it is also a part of honoring yourself.

Connect with others. Self-care involves healthy interaction with others in your life. You can't do your work or your life in isolation. The enemy of our souls will try to isolate you, so take deliberate action to connect with others inside and outside of work. Be proactive in cultivating friendships.

Every assistant needs the perspective and balance of a trusted friend or adviser when processing issues pertaining to work and ministry. Seek out a mature and trustworthy prayer partner for such times. Talk and pray with your leader about this need, and choose someone you both have confidence in. If you are married, do not assume this person is your spouse.

I can't stress enough the role of friends and family in how we take care of ourselves. I consistently surround myself with close friends and welcome their input, and I encourage all assistants to do the same.

Sabbath Rest

> *If we are not able to rest one day a week, we are taking*
> *ourselves far too seriously. Nothing less than a command*
> *has the power to intervene in the self-perpetuating cycle*
> *of faithless and graceless busy-ness.*
> —EUGENE PETERSON, *WORKING THE ANGLES*

All leaders and assistants tend to be very task-oriented people. The week doesn't seem long enough to address all that demands our attention. Jesus also experienced this when he ministered on earth. Yet, he took time to rest and be refreshed.

Marva Dawn, in her book *Keeping the Sabbath Wholly*, shares this: "God himself deliberately established a rhythm of six days of work and one day of ceasing work in order that our relationship with Him could reach greater depth."

Sabbath is a gift. It is designed to refresh us. For me it has been a wonderful relief to know that one day in every seven I can cease my work and relax. And this practice is blessed and consecrated by God.

Sabbath rest gives us not only refreshment but also new perspective, new priorities, and a renewed sense of God's presence. The Sabbath is not permission to run away from problems, but the opportunity to receive grace to face them.

So how do we slow down? How do we rest? No matter how busy you are, on Saturday evening (or whatever weekly day of rest you choose) stack your work, clear the desk, close the office door, and go home. In prayer, perhaps at bedtime, commit all the unfinished work into the Lord's hands. God will then show you how to enjoy true rest.

May your times of rest refresh you for times of service.

Friendship and Boundaries

To preserve healthy balance in your relationship with your leader, it is important to set boundaries between work and friendship times. This gives proper value to both.

I learned a good lesson about this several years ago when I was in Kona, Hawaii, helping to host the annual Mission CEO meeting. My leader, Peter, wanted to celebrate my birthday at breakfast with another leader. Because of Peter's travel schedule, I had not met with him for several days, so I came to breakfast with a list of things to discuss. I needed answers and direction to check these things off my list. If you are like me, you feel great satisfaction in checking off the items on your daily work list. But I left that time with my list unchecked. It was friendship time, not work time!

On another note, I have been intentional in building a friendship with Peter's wife, Luba, and she with me. We have enjoyed many lunches and prayer times together. Often Luba can help me in communicating with Peter, and she also helps Peter in communicating with me. She knows when to encourage me to take time off and has helped me set boundaries in serving her husband.

I strongly believe that assistants should not strive to become their leaders' best friends. This can lead to unhealthy expectations, burdening both leaders and assistants. While working together often leads to friendship with a leader, it doesn't in all cases. Having that expectation may lead to disappointment and discord.

The line between friendship and assisting can sometimes be blurred. As you see a need outside the office, determine your initial response with care. Knowing the need doesn't equal having to meet the need. For example, I noticed Peter and Luba's need for a nanny when their family traveled. However, I did not assume I was the solution during those times, and a suitable nanny was found.

Here are a few thoughts for you to ponder when it comes to friendship:

- Keep things resolved between you and the leader. "Don't let the sun go down on your anger" (Ephesians 4:26 HCSB).
- Talk through conflicts, remembering that your relationship affects others. When you disagree, show respect and honor both privately and publicly.
- Be inclusive. That means creating room for others to build relationships with your leader. There are times when assistants need to disappear.
- Other ministry people need access to your leader. Often a leader will schedule time with the leadership team or be invited out to play golf or attend special dinners with key leaders. Don't take offense if you are not included.
- Honor the leader's family. Do your part to ensure that the leader's spouse, children, and other family members have the best access.

Questions for Reflection

1. How does this topic of friendship and boundaries relate to your experience?
2. What does friendship between leaders and assistants look like in your culture?

KNOWING YOUR LEADER

*The example that the leader and assistant set with their
working relationship within the office also has a huge
impact on others within the office.*
—Elizabeth Hitchcock, executive assistant,
SIM International

Strengthening the Partnership

God has created us all uniquely. Leaders are no exception. To help make the partnership work well, we need to learn our leader's values, style of leadership, and giftings.

How does your leader process new ideas?

How does your leader problem solve?

How does your leader respond in a crisis?

What does your leader do under pressure?

What brings your leader stress?

Assistants must practice listening to their leaders to learn what values and issues are most important to them.

For example, I have heard Peter say again and again that he will do everything in his power to help equip younger leaders; he wants them to be better leaders than he is or ever will be. He makes room in his schedule to invest in them. Because of his words and actions, I know that equipping younger leaders is a key value for him.

Another definition for the word *partner* is "either of two people dancing together or playing a game or sport on the same side" (*New Oxford American Dictionary*). Think of partnership as learning what your leader's next step will be or anticipating your leader's next move so that you can be prepared to offer support.

I cannot emphasize enough how important it is to know your leader. You stand as an extension of the leader, often representing the leader to others.

There will be times when the leader will forget something or assume people know it already. This can happen in meetings and in correspondence. As the assistant, you can see whether people fully understand what your leader is trying to convey. Because you know your leader's values, you will be able to offer the missing piece. Keep your eyes and ears open. Is their communication effective? Are people hearing their passion? If you are in a public situation, discreetly offer any piece that might be missing by passing a note or pulling the leader aside at a break in the meeting. Never correct the leader in public. Once the leader is aware, they might choose to take care of the issue themselves or delegate it to you. The point here is to know the leader well enough to support them in their communication.

As your partnership grows, contribute ideas for better communication and problem solving. Your insights will make them a better leader. Of course, there will be times when you will have differences in perspective. Learn from these times, and honor and appreciate these differences.

Here are some practical questions about your leader that you need to be able to answer:

- How does your leader like to receive information about project details and deadlines—in person, by phone, or by e-mail? Sometimes you may need to press things a bit as a deadline nears. It might feel like you are nagging, but show your leader the big picture of why something is necessary at this time. As your partnership develops, you will learn when to yield and when to persist.
- Do you need to be available for impromptu meetings your leader may ask you to attend? Be in close proximity of the leader, as things may come up.
- How does your leader debrief after important trips or meetings? Help process action items that need follow-up.
- How does your leader process new visions? Verbally? Using a whiteboard? As visionaries, leaders sometimes appreciate processing out loud. Help by asking questions that clarify the vision.

New Vision and Ideas

When leaders bring in new vision or ideas, assistants tend to see more responsibilities. Though you may guard against taking on too much new responsibility, you must accept that helping your leader implement new direction is an important part of your assistant role. How you respond to the initial vision casting matters. Check your attitude and how it is expressed through body language, initial questions, and expressions.

Connect to the excitement of the big picture. You are on a team; you are serving a great God. Let the vision be spoken, let it get out there, see how it shakes down and what it becomes in the processing time. Don't immediately start arranging the details or determining how things can or can't be done. Allow the full development process to take place. Be as Mary is described in Luke 2:19, allowing time to listen and to ponder the vision. Carry it in your heart.

Support your leader in the vision. Receive it, and take the stance that it can be done. Know that the work is not just up to you. Remember that God works through teamwork.

Ask questions to help define the big picture and major goals. Ask about how your leader would like to be involved. What is the time frame? What resources are needed? Clarifying questions asked at the right time can bring a greater depth to the vision.

Remember that a leadership team most likely will be carrying out the new vision; your role is to assist the leader.

Questions for Reflection

1. What do you see that makes your leader unique among leaders you know?
2. What are some of your leader's giftings and strong beliefs?
3. How have you assisted your leader in defining and implementing new vision?

Representation: Reflecting Your Leader to Others

As an assistant, you are an extension of your leader and their position. You are a representative of the ministry's values and DNA. How you carry yourself and how well you serve others is a reflection of both your leader and the ministry. You will likely be designated to handle correspondence, phone calls, and direct conversations on your leader's behalf. Be careful not to add your own opinion in such communication; your job is to relay your leader's views. Always seek to reflect those values in your communication.

Here are a few practical points:

Be accessible. Leaders want to be available to coworkers, and part of their being accessible involves their assistants being accessible. Be easy to find or call. Welcome interruptions. Be visible at staff meetings.

Keep people connected to the leader in the leader's absence. When appropriate, pass on the leader's schedule and prayer requests.

Stay connected with the rest of the ministry. That may mean stepping outside your usual role for a few hours to help in the kitchen, mentor a new staff member, or do some form of outreach. Your connections with staff outside your office will bless you personally and will help bridge the distance between the leader's office and those it serves.

Refer to your leader with honor and respect in conversations, whether public or private. You may need to explain your leader's initiatives. Just as you had to process the vision, so will others. Your insights can help them understand the vision too.

Protect the integrity of others at all cost. Do not gossip.

Avoid all appearances of evil (1 Thessalonians 5:22). When meeting together, arrange to meet in public places. When traveling together, only do so with a third person, or consider traveling separately. At the office, take appropriate measures when meeting alone. Have windowed offices or doors, or keep the door ajar.

Be hospitable. Create an environment where others feel comfortable and cared for. When people are comfortable, they can get to the work at hand.

Access to the Leader

In all practicality, you are the access point to the leader. You have the opportunity to prioritize and make appointments. This powerful position brings up numerous challenges to your personal identity:

- A temptation of pride leading to control, in which you selfishly determine who gets access and when. You play favorites.
- A temptation to be defensive when facing disrespect and harassment by people who are aggressively seeking access to your leader.
- A temptation to respond competitively.

Therefore you must "trust in the LORD with all your heart and lean not on your own understanding" (Proverbs 3:5).

I recently received a call from a ministry leader asking to speak with Peter as soon as possible about a wonderful opportunity. I asked for a few details, but this person became very insistent and wanted to speak *only* with Peter. The caller had dismissed my role. I could have chosen to take it personally, become frustrated, and shut off all access to Peter. Instead, I thanked the person for calling our office and for considering a partnership with our ministry. This kind of response can defuse aggressiveness. I continued to ask questions to build connection. The caller hung up, assured that he had been heard, that the matter was important to us, and that it would get to Peter.

This was only a phone call. In a face-to-face situation things can feel more intense, but the same values still hold. I must not control the situation by dismissing someone. I must choose to defuse aggression and build up assurance that people are being heard and action will be taken.

Many times you might suspect that people will try to manipulate your leader's time. It is your job to guard, not to pass judgment on motives or a program or ministry. Represent all requests with integrity.

And finally, there is a temptation to react competitively, whether with other ministries or with coworkers. Ask yourself, "Am I okay with others going to my leader without asking me first? Do I think I am the only way in?"

When you're an assistant, lots of other ministries will approach you with excitement about their vision. Do you make a quick judgment call: Is their ministry valid? Are they a threat? Are they a competitor? Or do you keep yours ears and heart open, clinging to the value that the Lord desires to connect people and asking what he might being doing here?

As it turned out, the partnership proposed by the caller mentioned above did not happen, though it could lead to something in the future. The important thing is that people feel they have been heard and their ideas are valued. This keeps the door open for God to connect ministries and people. Many times you will be pleasantly surprised by how connections happen and fruit comes forth.

Remember that the enemy wants any in-road to sour relationships within the body of Christ. Your choices are a battlefield. Respond in grace, choosing to believe the best.

Handling Details

Assistants need to be able to recall situations, dates, phone conversations, and commitments; keep receipts and legal documents; and more. You will save a lot of time if you have the ministry's details organized in such a way that you can find them easily.

Develop your own system for keeping details using calendars, spreadsheets, and so on. (Some other ideas are listed in the Recommended Resources.) There are many ways to organize; choose one that works for you, and be committed to it. Consistent use of the system is key.

Here are some pointers:

- When taking notes, check with your leader to make sure facts are correct.
- In meetings with your leader, keep a running list of things that need to be done.
- Prioritize. Consider the amount of time needed to complete tasks before their due dates. Learn to discern the difference between major and minor items to bring to your leader.

- Avoid double-booking; remind your leader of what else they have on their schedule.
- Regularly back up your computer files.

In looking at your leader's schedule, anticipate the needs—for rest, family, study, project development, or meeting with staff who may need counsel or support but would not ask for it. Be flexible, as plans may need to change at the last minute. Do your best to implement necessary changes quickly, and be a self-starter when the leader is not there to give directions.

Only seek information needed to serve the leader better. You will be privy to sensitive information. Be trustworthy, and handle it with care. Understand levels of confidentiality. Some information may require passwords and lock and key; discuss this with your leader.

If you show confidence and prove yourself in this area of organization, your leader will be able to leave details to you and have peace of mind.

Questions for Reflection

1. What systems are working for you?
2. How do you keep information flowing?
3. What types of details might you need to remember or have access to?
4. How do you handle interruptions and schedule changes?

GUARDING YOUR LEADER

*Knowing that God entrusts us, jars of clay, with
amazing tasks of faith, why would I not guard
that with all my heart? It is not the leader only,
it is the stuff of God and his holy intentions that
are to be accomplished that I am jealous for.*
—KRISTEN JENSEN, YWAM

Being an Armor-Bearer

One of my very favorite accounts in the Bible is in
1 Samuel 14:1–23. This passage recounts the defeat
of the Philistines by Jonathan and his armor-bearer. Their
courageous act to challenge the enemy inspired the rest
of the army to put up a victorious fight. The agreement
between the armor-bearer and Jonathan mirrors the potential strength I see in the partnerships of assistants with
their leaders. Consider the armor-bearer's commitment in
1 Samuel 14:7:

"Do all that you have in mind," his armor-bearer said. "Go ahead; I am with you heart and soul."

The Hebrew meaning for "heart" in this verse is "inner man, resolution, determination, moral character, a seat of emotions and passions, a seat of courage" (*Strong's*).

We have to have heart.

The phrase "armor-bearer" translates into two Hebrew words: *nasa*, meaning "to lift, bear, carry away, give, help, hold up, pardon, respect, yield"; and *keliy*, meaning "to end, complete, be done, finish, and bring to pass" (*Strong's*).

The armor-bearer had counted the cost. This was no small thing, and it would potentially cost him all he had. His faith and the required risk matched that of his leader's. Contrast that with today's more familiar use of the word *heart* in phrases like "having a heart for," in which the word implies a strong interest or hope.

We need to set our hearts with determination, having a passion for our role as assistants. Is your heart daily activated to champion and guard your leader in this partnership? It will take a heart of courage and resolve to fulfill all that God has called you to.

The second aspect of the 1 Samuel story is the corporate blessing of Israel. Jonathan and the armor-bearer's commitment and determined action inspired those they represented. This can happen for you and your ministry as well.

At this point I want to touch on an issue not mentioned in staff training manuals. How do you respond when your leader reacts in fear or makes a significant mistake? You may be disappointed, especially if the leader has disregarded your advice. But guard your heart and be careful with your response. Being a great armor-bearer and assistant is about having the ability to see the human side of your leader and still maintain respect.

The Battle

> *The thief comes only to steal and kill and destroy; I have come that they may have life, and have it to the full.*
> —JOHN 10:10

This verse clearly reminds us that we have an enemy who doesn't want us to experience the abundant life of Jesus. Therefore, we will face battles in our ministries. One of our roles as armor-bearers is to watch out for and deflect some of these assaults on our leader. This is why it is imperative to take time daily with God. He will give us strength and perspective.

These battles or trials come from all directions, maybe even from within our own ministry. The challenges may come in the form of accusations, misunderstandings, unrealistic expectations, insecurities, and questions about the leader's integrity or motive.

The personal life of the leader is also vulnerable. Watch for attacks on the leader's marriage, children, health, and finances.

The enemy knows the vulnerabilities of your position, and he will try to poison your relationships or overwhelm you with matters that you, as an assistant, are not anointed to carry. I learned this the hard way. During a difficult time in YWAM, my position afforded me opportunities to hear the details of a painful situation. I could only listen. I internalized the struggle and wasn't consistently successful in giving the cares over to the Lord (1 Peter 5:7; Philippians 4:6–7).

I carried too much of this situation, and it became a burden, one too heavy for me to bear. The pressure affected my health, and the result was that I found myself in the emergency room. I was diagnosed with double pneumonia and forced to complete bed rest.

During that time, God showed me I was carrying too much of this particular situation and that I was not anointed to do so. I was not the North American Leader. I was his assistant. There are two different roles, two different anointings.

Even today I can feel the moment in which I might be crossing the line, and I remind myself of what the Lord taught me about my position. In all of this, I am not speaking of letting go of the sincere care for people involved; that is mine to carry. I am speaking of letting go of the pressure of my perceived responsibility to fix it.

It is not always an obvious evil or deep conflict that we face. Sometimes the battle is just plain busyness. Watch out for distractions, delays, or interruptions that are pulling you or the leader away from your focus. There will be times of peace, when all is running smoothly. Even then, we must be aware, standing alert to the fullness of what is to be taking place.

How do we fight these battles? It all starts with prayer. A watchman takes what he sees and reports to the king. The king then decides on a course of action. The watchman is only responsible for the report. In this illustration you are the watchman. Jesus is your king. Your prayers are your report. Look to him for the course of action.

Questions for Reflection

1. What battles or challenges do you face in your ministry?
2. Explore 1 Peter 5:7 and Philippians 4:6–7. How do these verses apply to your assisting?

Being a good assistant is an incredible task. Each of us has an important role. Every day is different. Enjoy the journey!

PART 2

LEADERS PARTNERING WITH ASSISTANTS

QUESTIONS TO GET THINGS GOING

1. What first comes to your mind when you think of having an assistant?

2. Do you have concerns about keeping an assistant busy or useful?

3. Begin thinking about what parts of your workload are too heavy for you to carry. What could you possibly give to an assistant to accomplish for you?

4. Consider the image of a tandem bicycle. How does this shape your thinking about your relationship with your assistant?

UNDERSTANDING PARTNERSHIP

*Leadership is the ability to decide what is to
be done and then get others to do it.*
—DWIGHT D. EISENHOWER, US GENERAL
AND THIRTY-FOURTH PRESIDENT

Partnership in Scripture

Throughout Scripture we see God using partnerships and teams to support leadership. We will begin our discussion of leaders partnering with assistants by looking at some of these examples of partnership.

Moses' father-in-law came for a visit (Exodus 18:13–23). Jethro observed that the demands of the people were creating a workload far too heavy for Moses to manage alone. He asks Moses, "Why do you alone sit as judge? . . . What you are doing is not good. You and these people who come to you will only wear yourselves out. The work is too heavy for you; you cannot handle it alone."

Jethro instructed Moses to delegate work, saying, "If you do this and God so commands, you will be able to stand the strain, and all these people will go home satisfied."

In the New Testament we see the same sort of leadership support. In Acts 6 as the number of disciples increased, the needs increased as well. Things were being overlooked. In order to address these needs, the leaders turned over responsibilities to others who were full of the Spirit and wisdom. The leaders did not neglect the ministry God had called them to.

"This proposal pleased the whole group" (verse 5). It was okay with the group that the leaders turned over work to others. And then there was fruit: "So the word of God spread. The number of disciples in Jerusalem increased rapidly" (verse 7).

Taking the concept further, recall the opening definition of the word *partner*: "a person who takes part in an undertaking with another or others with shared risks and profits." Can you see your assistant or administrative team in these terms?

We see specific partnerships between Moses and Aaron and Hur, Moses and Joshua, Paul and Timothy, Paul and Tychicus, and many others. Paul used scribes for his letter writing (Romans 16:22). For example, Tertius wrote the letter on paper, but the letter is authored and sent by Paul.

Scripture shows good working partnerships, which the Lord put together to fulfill his purposes. Your assistant is a potential ministry partner, an important complement to your work.

As a partner, your assistant is God's servant, committed to helping you succeed for the glory of the Lord. They can do—or find a way to get done—almost anything that you do not need to do personally. And they want to do it!

As you rely on the coworkers the Lord has given you to carry the weight of administrative tasks, you will be free to focus on the vision and future of the ministry.

Are you sorting the mail?

Are you doing the accounting?

Are you finding yourself making phone calls that an assistant could make?

Please don't miss out. My heart is that you, dear leader, will be free to lead. This freedom is gained by intentional investment of communication and time with your assistant.

May I encourage you to look at Jesus' example of how he worked with people? Even as a young boy, Jesus sat and listened and asked questions (Luke 2:46). As he went into ministry, he spent time with his team and ate with them. They had time to ask him questions. They had his attention, and he had theirs.

Listening, talking, asking questions . . . this is what makes partnering with assistants successful.

Questions for Reflection

1. In light of the definition of *partner* being "a person who takes part in an undertaking with another or others with shared risks and profits," how do you see your assistant sharing risks and profits?
2. Think through your responsibilities as a leader. In an honest evaluation, are there things you are neglecting? Could an assistant take care of these things for you?
3. Consider sitting down with an assistant to list your daily, weekly, and monthly responsibilities. Talk about

the assistant's giftings and what he or she might be able to do for you. The next chapter lists ways different types of assistants can partner with you.

KNOWING WHAT YOU NEED

There are many factors that could keep a leader from expanding their leadership capabilities, but consider this one thought: What about having them learn how to more effectively allow others to help them, and draw on their assistants' skills and gifts in a greater way?
—Ted Noble, former CEO of Greater Europe Mission

The Essential: Godly Character

Strong partnerships have multiple points of agreement. For leader-assistant partnerships in ministry, our beginning points of agreement lie in our character as followers of Christ. In Part 1 of this booklet, I have encouraged assistants to pursue the qualities listed in 1 Timothy 3:1–13.

Your assistant should be spiritually mature, trustworthy, gracious, servant-hearted, prayerful, teachable, patient, and committed to biblical standards, to your ministry's foundational values, and to open communication. Of course, no one is perfect, but we are all in the process of becoming like Christ, maturing in our faith.

Here are some specifics to look for in an assistant:

- A person of prayer and one of spiritual maturity with an obvious love for the Lord and his Word.
- One who rightly fears the Lord (Proverbs 9:10). Your assistant will be in a place of influence with you and in the ministry.
- A person who is committed and accountable to a local body of believers.
- A person who walks in humility and servanthood. This is not to be confused with insecurity. Look for someone who is confident in his or her role.
- One who values honest two-way communication. Find someone who is able to welcome and receive correction and input.
- One who demonstrates patience and walks in grace. You need someone who can walk alongside you through the various pressures and surprises in ministry.

Types of Assistants

What is needed for your ministry to move forward?

The Bible mentions many titles and roles: kings, servants, elders, deacons, and so on. Titles and roles carry with them different responsibilities and kinds of honor, authority, and anointing. They can be the basis of shared expectations.

Perhaps your ministry is more casual and so titles and job descriptions are seen as too formal or confining. We all want to preserve the value of relationship in ministry. However, the use of titles and roles is helpful in defining what is needed and who is responsible for meeting that need.

Here are a few titles that describe a variety of roles (these definitions will differ in various situations and cultures):

- *Personal assistant.* Provides support for the leader (usually of the same gender); travels with the leader; runs errands, including non-office-related tasks.
- *Clerical assistant (secretary).* Handles filing, data entry, general phone calls, and basic correspondence; this position is more mechanical and task oriented.
- *Administrative assistant.* Oversees and organizes the office, the schedule, and travel.
- *Executive assistant.* Anticipates the leader's needs, does follow-up regarding tasks and communication, prioritizes demands, keeps leader on task, and handles more private or sensitive information.
- *Project assistant.* Supports specific projects that have a defined goal and end point.
- *Accounting assistant.* Specializes in accounting and finance.

To this list we can add assistance by way of prayer and intercession. This is a more fluid role. It is essentially standing in a more concentrated role of prayer for a leader and the ministry. Sometimes those who are drawn to this way of assisting might not have strong administrative skills.

Beyond titles and job descriptions, it is good to know what you individually bring to the partnership. As you can see, all these roles cannot be effectively carried out by one person.

There are many tests that can help identify your gifts and strengths as well as those of your assistant (see Recommended Resources for suggestion). Once you have taken these tests, sit down and look at each other's results and discuss your differences and similarities. Find ways to help each other get your respective jobs done.

Questions for Reflection

1. What type of assistant do you feel would best partner with you?
2. What expectations do you have for working with an assistant?

GETTING THE WORK DONE

*Why leaders don't delegate: fear of losing authority, fear
of work being done poorly, fear of work being done better,
unwillingness to take the necessary time, fear of depending
on others, lack of leadership training and positive delegation
experience, fear of losing value in the organization.*
—HANS FINZEL, THE TOP TEN MISTAKES LEADERS MAKE

Communication with Your Assistant

The culture and times are changing. Many leaders don't
work in an office next door to the secretary every day.
This new type of distance puts tremendous pressure on a
team's ability to work together successfully. While communication technology has increased, it cannot replace the
value of face-to-face communication.

Clarity is key. Your assistant needs to know how best
to work with you. While many assistants can make an
educated guess, they cannot read your mind. The hours

you spend crafting your vision will result in corresponding hours of implementation for your assistant. Therefore, the point at which you begin to communicate the vision to your assistant is critical.

Mature assistants desire to help you. In order for assistants to have an accurate perception of their job, they must know your job and your goals for the ministry. Although they find purpose and fulfillment in taking care of details, they need to hear direction and vision for the week, month, and year.

Allowing assistants to observe your thinking and decision-making process will help them become more familiar with your goals and values.

Organization

Help your assistant help you by defining how to manage your projects, schedule, correspondence, travel, and more. Here are a few questions to consider:

- How would you like your appointments to be scheduled?
- What is the best way to remind you of appointments or deadlines? Is it your assistant's job to repeatedly remind you of an issue until it is resolved?
- How would you like to be kept up to date—verbally or in writing?
- How do you prefer to be contacted? E-mail? Text? Phone call?
- How do you want your assistant to handle interruptions while you are in a meeting?

- What kind of preparation is helpful for you before appointments, presentations, or trips?
- When will you and your assistant meet? Be aware of an assistant's tendency to schedule everyone else first, leaving inadequate time for you to meet together.

Representation

You have probably reminded your assistant that they are an extension of your ministry. Do they represent your voice as well? If so, tell your assistant when you want them to be speaking and acting on your behalf.

Are there times you expect your assistant to exercise authority over those directly under you? If so, make it clear when this is the case. Communicating with your assistant and others involved will ensure that your wishes are carried out smoothly.

With all good intentions, your assistant may not always represent your opinion the way you intend. Discern when your position needs to be restated and then inform your assistant first. They will appreciate hearing this from you first, not others. Give them an opportunity to express their perspective. They may have miscommunicated, but show respect by listening to their good intentions.

Additional Ideas for Effective Partnership

Here are some additional considerations for developing effective partnerships:

Project tracking. One of the best ways an assistant can serve you is by tracking projects so you can focus on something else. Your assistant can also help you track progress on work you have delegated to others. At a designated time, your assistant can report on what was done and what is yet to be done.

Travel. When traveling, take the initiative to phone your assistant to provide updates and receive messages. This will help prevent interruptions of your meetings and conversations. Debrief with each other as soon as possible after travel or important meetings, either in person or by phone or e-mail if you are away from the office.

Networking. Introduce your assistant to key people. Include your assistant in meetings and social events at which they can connect with people they will likely communicate with later.

Discretion. If your assistant is of the opposite sex, arrange to meet in public places. When traveling together, only do so with a third person. At the office, take appropriate measures when meeting alone. Have windowed offices or doors, or keep the door ajar. Those in ministry leadership must be especially careful to avoid all appearances of evil (1 Thessalonians 5:22). Consider asking your spouse to befriend your assistant (when they are the same gender). Encourage them to enjoy meals and prayer times together. Your spouse can also help your assistant communicate with you and help you communicate with your assistant.

Scheduling priorities. Discuss your ministry, family, and personal priorities. An assistant wants to champion your family and can spot (possibly more quickly than you) conflicting appointments. Also, if an activity like going to the gym refreshes you, have your assistant schedule it as a regular appointment.

Questions for Reflection

1. Review Hans Finzel's statement about fears in delegation at the beginning of this section. Do you have any of the fears he lists?
2. What habits or mind-sets could you change to help you release or overcome these fears?
3. With your assistant, review the questions in the "Organization" section. What other important questions could you answer for your assistant?

THINKING FORWARD

[Love] always protects, always trusts,
always hopes, always perseveres.
—1 Corinthians 13:7

Training and Effectiveness

Take time with your assistant to evaluate your current office situation. Are things running well? Are deadlines being met? Are there times during the year when the workload is overwhelming? Are there tasks that can be eliminated? Is there a need for division of labor? Work together to pinpoint areas needing improvement.

For example, our office does not need a full-time accountant, so for a while I was handling our finances. Handling the bank statements and other accounting details became overwhelming. So my leader, Peter, and I reviewed the amount of time I devoted to accounting every month and decided my time was better spent on other tasks. We now have a part-time accountant.

While no one wants increased overhead, you can often save time and money by reassigning tasks or giving your staff additional training and more efficient tools. Consider these questions: Are there additional tools, such as software or updated equipment, that will help them get their jobs done more effectively? What additional training would help your staff? Have you read any books or articles that would be helpful to pass on to your staff?

Peter has always encouraged and released me to attend training workshops and seminars. He recognizes that these times are an important investment. I traveled to Egypt to attend a three-week seminar taught by the founders of our mission. I learned more about the history and foundational values of our mission, which has helped me understand the big picture while working on specific projects.

It is important to increase your assistant's responsibilities as they grow with the job. If they are doing well, take some time to acknowledge this and talk with them about the future. Identify their strengths and weaknesses: ask what ignites them and what depletes them. Based on their input, assign additional responsibilities accordingly.

Encourage your assistant's participation in forming strategies and solutions. Request that they attend meetings with you (or for you) to listen, record, and observe. Then debrief together.

Consider involving your assistant in researching and drafting more of your communication, including letters, e-mails, teachings, and seminar presentations.

You can help chart your assistant's abilities and growth by providing annual development reviews. Examine their accomplishments and growth. Point out where they can take on more responsibilities, and discuss which areas to concentrate on more intentionally. Encourage them to set annual goals that are measurable, both professionally and personally.

Affirmation and Appreciation

Does your assistant know when a job is well done? Acknowledge and thank them for their work, especially if they are volunteers. To reinforce their role in the ministry, consider bringing back photos or small gifts from places where you travel. Encouragement helps build trust and respect into your partnership.

Another form of honor is to compliment your assistant in front of others. They will feel humbled and maybe embarrassed, but they will feel valued. We all need to feel valued in our work.

I remember a time that Peter presented me with a dozen long-stemmed red roses at a conference in front of more than 250 leaders. I was embarrassed, yes, but it was a great surprise and blessing too. I felt so honored and appreciated by him and all the others.

Caring for Your Assistant

The position of assistant holds unique pressures. Assistants are fully aware of their leaders' intentions and responsibilities in ministry. They are also aware of the activities of the ministry and its people. Many times assistants feel caught between these two worlds. By recognizing this, you can help your assistant keep perspective.

Your assistant most likely is driven to see tasks accomplished. A fully checked-off list brings a sense of completion and inspires further work. On the other hand, assistants may feel stress about unfinished work. It is not always easy for assistants to stop working; they tend to want to resolve all outstanding matters before bedtime. Of course, that isn't possible every day. If your assistant is unable to live with this reality, it can cause burnout.

Consider some ways to care for your assistant:

Maintain a good sense of humor. Encourage yourselves to not take each other too seriously. Laughter adds a new dimension to teamwork.

Pass on information. When possible, provide your assistant with context and detail to eliminate guesswork and make things more efficient.

It is sometimes necessary to remind your assistant to take a break, a vacation, or a spiritual retreat. An assistant who is constantly tired cannot serve you well.

Consider a yearly evaluation time. Take the opportunity to hear your assistant's perspective on how the partnership is going.

Encourage your assistant to have a prayer partner—a person with maturity and experience who will keep a good perspective and maintain confidentiality, both crucial for the ministry. Having an avenue for processing things will keep your assistant's outlook healthy. Some burdens are too heavy to carry alone. A prayer partner will alleviate the temptation to complain, gossip, and grumble.

Encourage your assistant to travel and see ministry locations and connect with other organizations. This will enable them to know how their work is helping fulfill the vision of the ministry as a whole. It will also strengthen the sense of partnership between you, for when they see what you see, they will be able to assist you better.

Whenever possible, cover an unintended mistake or offense as a show of support for your assistant. One time I made a mistake in the way I communicated something to another leader. Peter called the person and took responsibility for the misunderstanding. That made me want to work all the harder to affirm his trust in me. He has provided shade for me many times.

Provide protection for your assistant when they need it, and when all goes well, make sure your assistant receives the credit due.

> *Above all, love each other deeply, because love cov-*
> *ers over a multitude of sins. Offer hospitality to one*
> *another without grumbling. Each of you should use*
> *whatever gift you have received to serve others, as*
> *faithful stewards of God's grace in its various forms.*
> *If anyone speaks, they should do so as one who speaks*
> *the very words of God. If anyone serves, they should do*
> *so with the strength God provides, so that in all things*
> *God may be praised through Jesus Christ. To him be*
> *the glory and the power for ever and ever. Amen.*
> —1 PETER 4:8–11

Questions for Reflection

1. With your assistant, review the questions at the beginning of the "Training and Effectiveness" section.
2. Make a mental list of ways you could show your appreciation to your assistant. As you work together, keep adding to your list.

WHO'S PACKING YOUR PARACHUTE?

The following story comes from Captain Charlie Plumb, former Navy fighter pilot and POW.*

Recently, I was sitting in a restaurant in Kansas City. A man about two tables away kept looking at me. I didn't recognize him. A few minutes into our meal he stood up and walked over to my table, looked down at me, pointed his finger in my face and said, "You're Captain Plumb."

I looked up and I said, "Yes sir, I'm Captain Plumb."

He said, "You flew jet fighters in Vietnam. You were on the aircraft carrier *Kitty Hawk*. You were shot down. You parachuted into enemy hands and spent six years as a prisoner of war."

I said, "How in the world did you know all that?"

He replied, "Because, I packed your parachute."

* From www.charlieplumb.com. Used by permission.

I was speechless. I staggered to my feet and held out a very grateful hand of thanks. This guy came up with just the proper words. He grabbed my hand, he pumped my arm and said, "I guess it worked."

"Yes sir, indeed it did," I said, "and I must tell you I've said a lot of prayers of thanks for your nimble fingers, but I never thought I'd have the opportunity to express my gratitude in person."

He said, "Were all the panels there?"

"Well sir, I must shoot straight with you," I said. "Of the eighteen panels that were supposed to be in that parachute, I had fifteen good ones. Three were torn, but it wasn't your fault, it was mine. I jumped out of that jet fighter at a high rate of speed, close to the ground. That's what tore the panels in the chute. It wasn't the way you packed it."

"Let me ask you a question," I said. "Do you keep track of all the parachutes you pack?"

"No," he responded, "it's enough gratification for me just to know that I've served."

I didn't get much sleep that night. I kept thinking about that man. I kept wondering what he might have looked like in a Navy uniform—a Dixie cup hat, a bib in the back and bell bottom trousers. I wondered how many times I might have passed him on board the *Kitty Hawk*. I wondered how many times I might have seen him and not even said "good morning," "how are you," or anything because, you see, I was a fighter pilot and he was just a sailor. How many hours did he spend on that long wooden table in the bowels of that ship weaving the shrouds and folding the silks of those chutes? I could have cared less . . . until one day my parachute came along and he packed it for me.

Everybody needs someone to pack their parachute. We all need those who will step out in front and say, "Yes, I'll help."

In God's service there are a variety of tasks. All of us need to work together to complete the job.

RECOMMENDED RESOURCES

Recommended Reading

Boundaries: When to Say Yes, How to Say No to Take Control of Your Life by Dr. Henry Cloud and Dr. John Townsend

Catch Your Breath: God's Invitation to Sabbath Rest by Don Postema

God's Armor Bearer, Vol. 1 & 2: Serving God's Leaders by Terry Nance

God's Armor Bearer, Vol. 1 & 2, 40-Day Study by Terry Nance

The Hamster Revolution: How to Manage Your Email Before It Manages You by Mike Song, Vicki Halsey, and Tim Burress

Leading with a Limp: Take Full Advantage of Your Most Powerful Weakness by Dan B. Allender

Managing Up: How to Forge an Effective Relationship with Those Above You by Rosanne Badowski

Sabbath (The Ancient Practices Series) by Dan B. Allender

The Top Ten Mistakes Leaders Make by Hans Finzel (especially chapter 6, "Dirty Delegation")

Websites and Software

RegOnline.com is great for online registration for group events.

Lynda.com has a library of over a thousand video courses on software, business, and creative skills.

Resources for Discovering Strengths

The book *Strengths Finder* by Tom Rath (www.strengthsfinder.com)

The website *Inspirational Leadership: Insight to Action* (www.inspiredleadership.org.uk)

ACKNOWLEDGMENTS

Thanks to those who contributed to this project:

YWAM: Peter Iliyn, Jean Elmlund, and Dawn Gauslin
GEM: Ted Noble and Kathy Griffith
C&MA: Loretta Nelson
World Venture: Joyce McCollum
SIM: Elizabeth Hitchcock
Navigators: Marjie Barnes, Kathy Fortner, and Lacy Muth

I want to thank the Christian Renewal Center near Silver Creek Falls in Oregon for their hospitality and for opening up a room for me to work on this booklet. Visit their website at *christianrenewalcenter.org*.

A special thanks to Kristen Jensen, who spent hours with me working on the manuscript. Her experience in ministry and assisting leaders for twenty-five years was invaluable in completing the project.

I want to recognize and thank Scott Tompkins with YWAM for helping edit this booklet. Scott, you did more than just this—you challenged me to add some great points I had not covered. Thank you!

A heartfelt thanks to the staff at YWAM Publishing for your encouragement and your commitment to this project. Thanks to Ryan Davis, who was an excellent editor, and to Angela Bailey for her cover design work.

Please e-mail your comments or questions to Karen Hawkins at leadersandassistants@gmail.com